Approved by LEO

The finest seal of approval based on taste, looks and durability. All done by my son Leo at 1,5 years old.

ISBN

ISBN-13: 978-91-980904-6-8

CONTACT INFO

Skyborn Works, Lyckselevagen 38, LGH 1102. 162 67 Vallingby. SWEDEN.
T: +46 73 649 83 11
contact@skybornworks.com

www.futurelittle.com
www.skybornworks.com

THRIFT STORE

VINTAGE CLOTHING

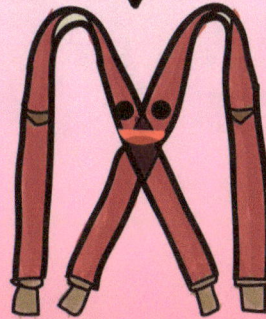

IRONIC T-SHIRT

HEADWEAR

KITSCH ACCESSORIES

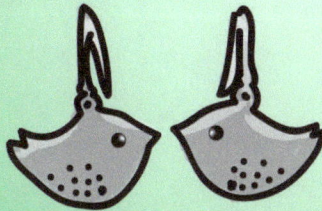

IRONIC EYEWEAR

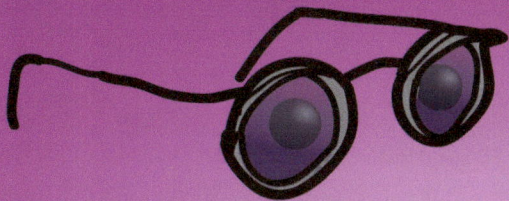

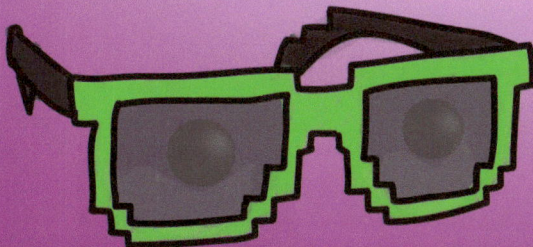

LEATHER BAGS

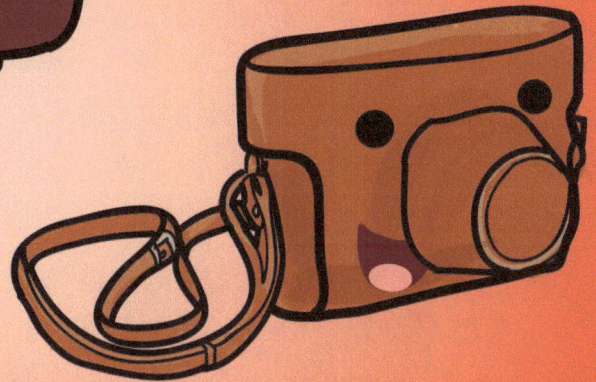

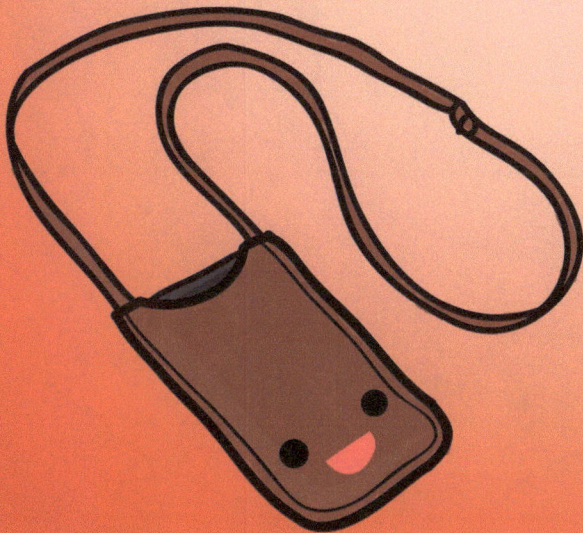

TRENDY GADGETS

FIXIE

ANALOG CAMERAS

TATTOOS

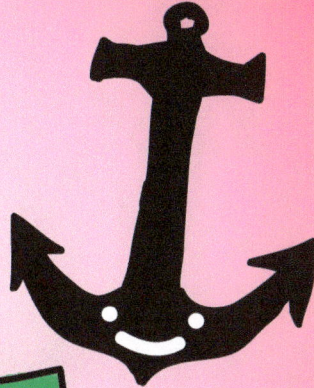

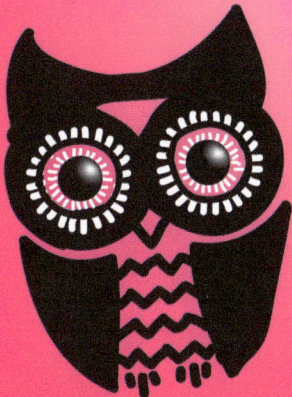

ORGANIC PRODUCTS

URBAN FARMING

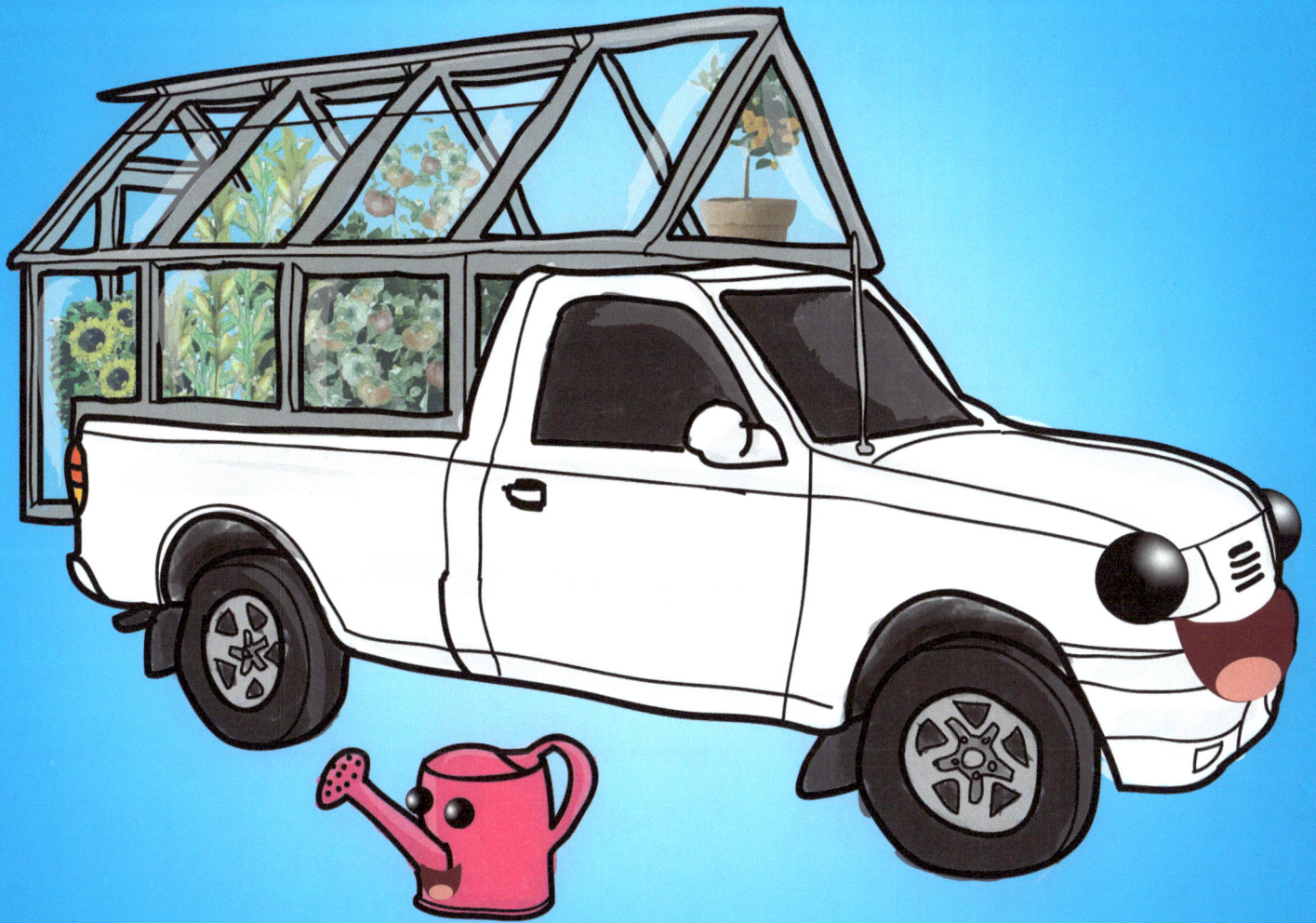

HIPSTER COFFEE

MICROBREWING

IRONIC MUSTACHE

HIPSTER
BEARD

INDIE MUSIC

WIFI JUNKIE

MEMES

MICROBLOGGING

KNITTING

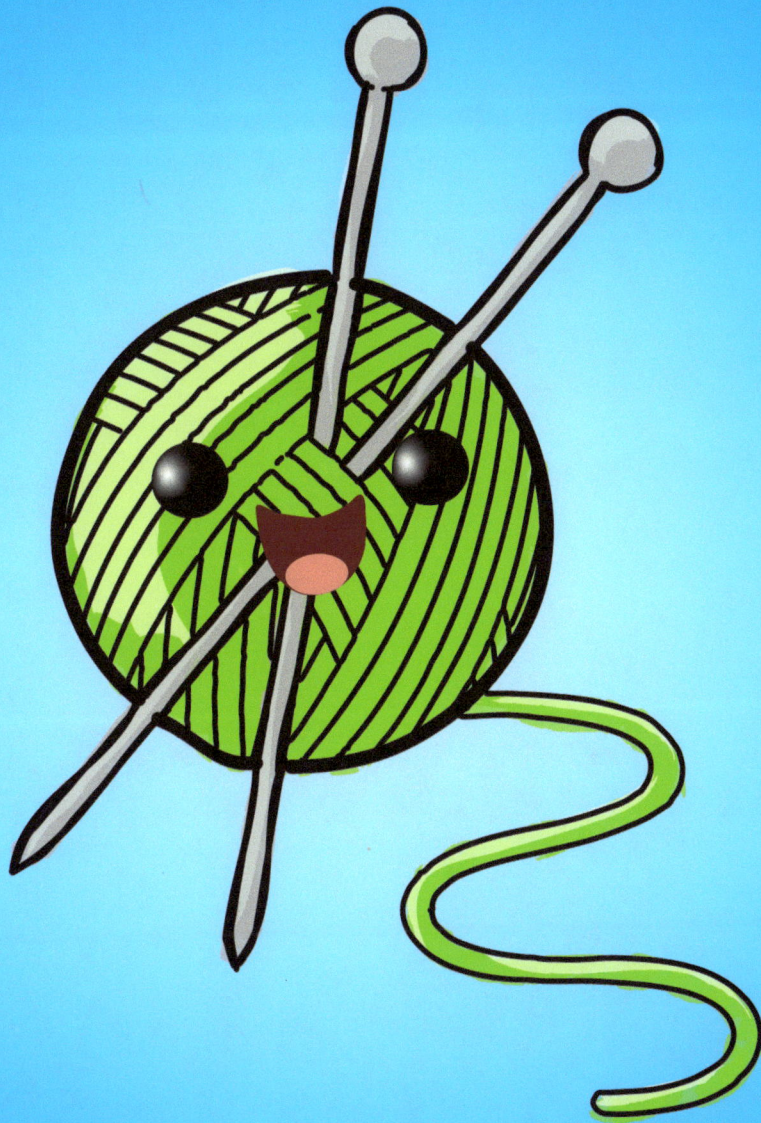

www.ingramcontent.com/pod-product-compliance
Lightning Source LLC
Chambersburg PA
CBHW042059040426
42448CB00002B/74